PILGRIMS OF THE NIGHT

Len Jenkin

BROADWAY PLAY PUBLISHING INC
224 E 62nd St, NY, NY 10065
www.broadwayplaypub.com
info@broadwayplaypub.com

THE PEOPLE

POOR TOM, *the ferry terminal caretaker*
MR SAMUEL SUNDOWN, *a prophet, in his way*
LILY BLACK, *a reporter and adventuress*
RAY T FOX, *a businessman*
VIVA, *the ferry captain's wife*
PROFESSOR HUBERT, *a performer*
ZOE, *his assistant*

THE TALES

THE STORY OF NICK SLICK, DARLENE, RUDY,
  AND GEORGE THE COOK—*told by* RAY
AT THE ZOMBIE JAMBOREE—*told by* LILY
DR KREMSER, VIVISECTIONIST—*told by* SAMUEL
OLGA, THE HEADLESS WOMAN—*told by* VIVA
THE STORY OF ELMO MARCH—*told by* ZOE
THE ADVENTURES OF BUNNY AND DICK—*told by*
  HUBERT

There is only the goal, no way. What we call the way is hesitation.
Franz Kafka

In the air men shall be seen
In white, in black, and all in green.
The Prophecies of Mother Shipton, 1641

With apologies to
Geoffrey Chaucer and Herman Melville

ACT ONE

(A ferry terminal in the north, on the bank of a wide river. The building is old and not in the best condition. It seems to handle light traffic at best—some of the place is under repair, and there are only a few benches and chairs. There is one door on a side wall that leads to the outside, and at the far end is the ferry boarding entrance. In one portion of the terminal is a small handmade living area: a raggedy couch that could be used for sleeping, a lamp, a chair. There is a radio communications rig and a large speaker. A large sign or boarding arrow indicates a ferry is in: "TO ALL FERRIES—BOARDING".)

(The terminal can be intersected in space by elements of a sort of dream cabinet: doors, windows, and decor that are from the realm of the stories told rather than the realm of the terminal. Microphones on stands for use when necessary or interesting. It's a ferry terminal—and a theater for the tales to come.)

(MR SAMUEL SUNDOWN is asleep on a bench in the terminal. He wears a dark suit, much the worse for wear.)

(POOR TOM, a young man in work clothes, is waiting for the ferry to leave so he can begin the play. It does. A horn sounds, and a clanging of bells. The sign changes, indicating the ferry's gone to cross the river.)

(We hear the ferry horn again, this time from a distance. TOM turns to the audience.)

TOM: Poor Tom is what they call me here. My job is to work the loading ramp, check weather, sell tickets, and be pleasant to anyone who gets this far. This far north. We are on the banks of the river, on a dirt road about twenty miles from High Point, which is the name for a clearing in the woods by a railroad platform.

A few years ago they kicked me off a freight down there. I hadn't eaten for three days. I had got myself so lost in this world I no longer knew who I was, much less where I was going. I just stumbled in among the trees and kept on.

Somehow I made it to the river bank. The river was talking. It said, "Hey buddy, you are a man who ought to drown yourself." That made perfect sense to me, and I was taking off my shoes when I saw the ferryboat out in midstream. It looked like a toy, all white, with a thin streak of smoke floating over the stack. Then the Captain hit the horn. That sound went through and through me. I beat along shore, following the boat. They found me in the woods behind the terminal, too shy and raggedy to come in. Now I live here. Poor Tom, at your service.

(SAMUEL *rises from his sleep.*)

TOM: The river is wide, deep and fast. There's no bridge over it for two hundred miles in either direction. If you're going over, you take this ferry.

It's my part here to let you know...

SAMUEL: The boat? It's gone...

TOM: You fell asleep.

SAMUEL: Indeed. The boat...

TOM: In the morning, if the weather's right.

SAMUEL: Good. That's good. Thank you.

TOM: It's my part here to let you know who all the...

ACT ONE

SAMUEL: I got the word three days ago. This earth is rolling, wiggle-waggle. It's rocking in its orbit. A farmer told me his sheep tore a timber wolf to pieces.

TOM: If you'd just *wait*, till I...

SAMUEL: A deer came out of the woods to look at me, and he was covered with horrible burns, puffy blisters oozing. His eyes looked so big and sad. Every night I've seen stars fall from the sky.
This morning a crow lands on my shoulder and he weeps. Black bird tears burned a hole in my shirt. Invisible worlds have linked arms, and they're going out dancing.
Something's gonna follow. First the fire, then the rain. Hear it?

(There is a sound of light rain that's come up under...)

SAMUEL: A priest in Rock City, his gall bladder exploded. Woman told me she caught her tomcat in the yard, trying to fuck a skunk. The river runs backwards to its source, and...

TOM: Bullshit. This river runs true, right down to the sea.

(Sound of car arriving outside, slamming of door. Car pulls away. LILY BLACK *appears in the doorway. Light rain is heard outside as she enters.)*

SAMUEL: Poor Tom's got company.

LILY: I did, didn't I? I missed the boat.

TOM: Yes, ma'am. But that's O K.

LILY: You being sarcastic?

TOM: No. There's nothing over there but a terminal like this one, woods all around. There's not much of a trail leading away. You don't want to go bushwack in the dark.

LILY: You trying to talk sense to me? Good luck.

TOM: There's a boat in the morning, if the weather's right.

LILY: What?

SAMUEL: I heard it on the news. Gonna be wet. High water. Everything else so lively, you think the river gonna stay in its bed?

LILY: Who is this character?

TOM: I'm trying to get to that…

SAMUEL: Wild night at the ferry.

LILY: Really? Is there a Burger King anywhere around here? Econolodge? A clean pile of straw?

SAMUEL: I walked from High Point, and there's nothing on either side of that dirt road but pine trees, broken glass, and raccoon shit. This is it.

(TOM *again gets in position to address the audience.*)

TOM: When strange and powerful events occur, people are drawn to them. They leave their dinner on the fire and the lights on, and they don't remember to turn the coffee off, and they go. People gather round a train wreck, an appearance of the Blessed Virgin, an outbreak at the lunatic asylum, a dead whale on the beach, an eclipse of the sun. Something in them stirs. Three nights ago a great ball of fire flashed through the night sky. The Captain and Viva and me ran outside and looked up at it. It seemed to stop and start again, and then it just hung there over the river. It was like another moon, but brighter, with lights inside itself that kept dancing and changing. The Captain was grinning like he couldn't stop. He lit his pipe and kept saying, "Well, what do you know." The whole river was glistening. Viva just sipped her tea.

ACT ONE

Then it fell, on a long arc north. There was a sound like thunder, and a red glow lit the sky, low on the horizon. It crashed, or maybe it landed, somewhere on the far side of the river. They talked about it on the radio, and Viva told me we'd get some traffic—light, but interested.

They missed the boat, the river's rising, and the weather's foul. They'll all stay here tonight. It's my part to let you know who all the travellers are, their names and occupations, and to give you some idea of how they think and what about.

This young lady's Lily Black, a city girl who knows what's up, what's down, what's new, and where to get it. She's in the galleries, the clubs, the bars. She knows some lunatic poets and some movie stars.

LILY: Kevin is just a friend…

TOM: On her left ass cheek, by the way, is a tattoo of a seahorse with the word "Remember" in some flowy script below.

Of course, her love life is a mess. She's living with a stockbroker named Robert, who seems to have more money than the Pope. Her old flame is a biker named Sundog, and she still rides with him when he's in town.

LILY: They're both jerks. Have you got any kind of vending device?

TOM: Sorry. There's food on the ferry. I used to have a snack stand—hot dogs, drinks. I even baked pies. Viva helped me set it up, but not enough people came through to make it pay.

LILY: I wonder why.

TOM: Lily's been to every sacred spot, megalith to medicine wheel. She's looking for something, and she's found a way to make her looking pay. She writes about it in the Monkey's Mirror.

LILY: A journal of contemporary culture and astro-archeology. The French edition's *Le Miroir du Singe*. You seen it?

SAMUEL: I haven't had the privilege.

TOM: They sent her here to write about an Indian burial mound.

LILY: They say it glows...every now and then.
I was at the train window, watching that forest go by forever...and I missed my stop, and the conductor is yelling High Point, end of the line.
They made me get off the train. Dirt road to nowhere. I hear a horn, and a guy drives up with a foot-high pompadour in a 1949 Buick Starfire, and the word TAXI is painted on the side in tractor enamel. He invites me to view the inside of his trailer, which is up above the station in a clearing surrounded by auto parts. I tell him I have a gun and no thanks, and then he says, "You must be the first." I say, "First what?" "First to come see where it landed," and he tells me about this flaming doughnut that sailed over a few nights ago.
I don't think *Monkey's Mirror* will mind if I come back with a saucer exclusive. Here I am.

TOM: Mister Samuel Sundown is an ex-hustler, and an ex-porno film star. He's an ex-panhandler, an ex-fry cook, and an ex-Trappist monk. They took him into the order, and he kept the vow of silence, worked the fields, and prayed for seven years. Then he rifled the cash register at the jam works, apologized to the abbot in a nicely worded note, and hopped a bus. Now he's unemployed. He keeps himself extremely clean, depends on public assistance, and spends his days in

ACT ONE

libraries, doing the sort of private study that always got him into trouble in the first place.

SAMUEL: Mention my book.

TOM: There's a book, all about how this connects with that, and certain proofs of certain holy mysteries. This book exists only in Mister Samuel Sundown's mind.

SAMUEL: I have writer's block.

TOM: His years with the Trappists burned his insides out somehow. His health is shot. Something with the lungs. He won't see a doctor. They all tell him he should go to the hospital.

SAMUEL: Assholes. When there is a sign in the heavens, do you think about adventures for your penis and watch T V? Or do you rise up and follow? That's all I have to say. Right now.

LILY: What's that shell you're wearing?

SAMUEL: Scallop.

TOM: Why do you wear it?

SAMUEL: It means I am a pilgrim. On my way to the cathedral of Saint James at Compostella. In Spain. Compostella means field of stars. Of course, I am not actually going there. It's the idea. I'm going across the river in the morning.

(Sound of a car, sweeping lights of a big limousine from outside. RAY T FOX *appears in the doorway. He wears a rock and roll tour jacket. Wind, thunder, rain as he enters)*

CHAUFFEUR'S VOICE: *(From outside. Screaming through the storm)* Mister Fox? When do I...

RAY: *(Yelling back outside)* I don't know when, Charlie! I'll call.

(Engine roar, sweep of headlights pulling away)

RAY: I miss the cruise?

TOM: Next boat's in the morning, if the weather's right.

RAY: That's fine, my friend. I don't mind waiting. Not one bit.

TOM: Ladies, and gentlemen, the charming Mister Ray T Fox. He's got the ideas, and he's got the nerve. Ray's made his own way in the world since he was twelve years old, shining shoes and stealing cars. He's a man on the move. He's a film producer...

RAY: But I don't make those slasher films anymore. In the end, you gotta think, who is it that's viewing the product? Is it Albert Einstein? Unlikely. It is every lowlife moron with five bucks. They watch *Death in the Dorms* and they don't think, "Hey, funny flick, nice chicks." They think, "So that's how a girl's head looks on a stick..."

TOM: These new scruples slow the cash flow, so Ray is branching out. He's an agent, a promoter, and has some connection with a mining business.

RAY: Hey, fella.

TOM: Yeah.

RAY: You're making me sound bad. You're doing it on purpose, O K. Working here on the loading ramp make you Mother Teresa? I got a two-pack habit and a motel tan. I'm not Paul Bunyan, O K. No crime. I'm on a highly competitive business track, O K. No crime. I do represent the Black Rapids Uranium Company, and it doesn't get any more legitimate. In fact, they have extensive interests in this very area. Mining rights to about fifty thousand acres on the other side of the river. I handle sales of letter stock in the firm, prior to public issue. I'm not here on Black Rapids business, but, if any of you are interested, we can talk.
I left a U-Haul parked outside. Can I get a hand bringing a few things onto the boat tomorrow?

ACT ONE 9

TOM: Can I ask what I'm gonna be carrying?

RAY: Sunglasses, toaster ovens, D V Ds, toothpaste, beads. Trade goods.

SAMUEL: You think those woods are full of Mohicans? Kwakiutl? That's insane.

RAY: Is it? 'Zere a Coke machine?

LILY: Nothing.

RAY: When the love boat leaves the dock, we'll stand at the rail, and when the yellow moon sinks into the sea, and the first breeze of twilight stirs your white lace dress around your thighs, I'll be there for you. My cabin is your cabin.

LILY: Fuck off.

RAY: You think I'm a conniving bag of bullshit, don't you?

LILY: You got it.

RAY: The night is young.

(The ferry terminal door opens again, strong wind and rain. VIVA *enters. She's soaked by the storm, and she's in a hurry.)*

VIVA: Tom, he leave yet?

TOM: On time.

VIVA: And you let him go. Two grown men can't turn on a radio? Look up at the sky, maybe you'd notice, hey the sky's *black*, and the wind's ripping the leaves off the trees… *(Noticing the new arrivals, and the audience)* Excuse me. I'll be right back. *(She heads for the radio communications unit.)*

TOM: That's Viva.

*(*VIVA *makes a call.)*

TOM: Only place that phone calls is a terminal just like this one—on the other side of the river.

(VIVA's *talking softly into the phone.*)

TOM: Viva and the Captain live in that small yellow house just down the road. She's a dancer. Once a year she disappears for six weeks. She dances in cities somewhere. She goes to the movies, stays in hotels, and speaks strange languages. She buys books and coffee and wine. Then she comes back, loaded with packages, and all her dancing is in the meadow, with the trees.

(VIVA *hangs up the phone.*)

VIVA: The Captain doesn't travel. He fishes the river in a little dinghy, and he walks along the shore. He's got a telescope, and boxes full of old books. I love him, I think. Most days.

TOM: Viva didn't want this life. She wanted the Captain, and the life was his.

VIVA: The crossing was rough. No way he can come back tonight. He'll sleep on the other side and try to make it over after its light.

RAY: What's the word? On the fireball?

LILY: We hear a lot of stories...

VIVA: So do we. The Captain's checking into it. He'll call back later. *(To all, and audience)* Why don't you all relax and...

(Lights flicker...)

VIVA: Tom? What's happenning with the lights?

TOM: *(Shrugs)* They haven't been right for days.

VIVA: Dark or light, make yourselves at home. You might as well. You're here till morning, when the boat

ACT ONE

arrives. Let your life recede—just float it on the river and let it bob away.

(A huge peal of thunder)

VIVA: I'm staying right here myself, as I don't like sleeping in an empty bed, and no one wants to drown on their way home.

(A lightning flash, and then the lights go out.)

(In the darkness, we see the door open, and two figures appear in silhouette. One is a man in a cape, and the other, a smaller companion. The door closes behind them, and we are again in more complete darkness. Sound of a drum)

HUBERT: Whatever creatures you are, hidden in darkness, be not afraid. Fortune has smiled on your den. From this moment, your life will be filled with wonders.

RAY: Hold onto your wallets.

(Scurrying and chaos in the dark, strange bells, a flash of fire)

LILY: Hey, keep your hands off me.

HUBERT: Zoe! Leave them alone.

(We can hear ZOE's laughter in the dark.)

TOM: What...get away from...who's that??

SAMUEL: Wha... Little imp...

(ZOE laughs again.)

(The lights flicker, finally come back on. People's clothes are askew, RAY's pockets turned inside out. The newcomers: HUBERT is in a raggedy suit, with a magician's cape the worse for wear and the weather. ZOE is not more than eighteen and dressed in odd pants and an odder hat. A small drum hangs off her.)

HUBERT: Where've you been in the dark, Zoe darling?

ZOE: Fishing, but there's not a lot to hook in these waters.

SAMUEL: Nero's child, isn't she?

HUBERT: He may be the emperor of this world, sir, but every girl's not his daughter.

TOM: PROFESSOR HUBERT AND THE AMAZING ZOE!

(As HUBERT gives the following speech, ZOE plays the drum for dramatic effect.)

HUBERT: Zoe and I have arrived, direct from performances before the crowned heads of Europe, including Princess Stephanie of Monaco, before whom we performed the unforgivable Wheel of Death. Before the crowned heads of Africa, including the King of Togo, who weighs over four hundred pounds and carries a golden cup, we performed the singular Mystery of the Seven Doves. I'd be pleased to offer you a sample of our skill, but all our apparatus was lost in a storm at sea.

ZOE: Overboard.

(LILY goes to HUBERT, looks him over.)

LILY: Your beard's a fake, and your eyebrows are dyed black.

HUBERT: For the public. Does Professor Hubert of vaudeville, the chatauqua, T V, and the Satellite Cocktail Lounge have less right to gild the lily than any schoolgirl?

RAY: You two done T V?

ZOE: We had our own special. Kind of a late-night thing.

HUBERT: A half hour of magic and wacky comedy.

ACT ONE

ZOE: We never should have done that shit. I don't like working indoors.

TOM: Hubert had another life once, but he's left it so far behind it can't reach him, even if it tries. A letter can't find him—no address. No phone. No driver's license. No magic act. They don't have one. They sell things.

HUBERT: Let me introduce you all to Zoe. She plays drums, sells tickets, and she does the ankle catch when we work under canvas.
I rescued her from a life of shame. She was working Melanie's Chicken Ranch outside of Elko...a teen runaway, brutal family in Minneapolis, and I was entertaining at the AIDS hospice at the time. She attached herself to me, forcefully.
I actually found her in a vacant lot, rehearsing a dog act she made from strays she got at the pound.

ZOE: Arf.

HUBERT: To be frank, good people, Zoe's my niece, and since her parents died in that tragic accident at Disneyland, she helps me with my simple stage machines. That's the truth. *(To* TOM*)* Does that cover it?

TOM: Thanks for the help. Professor Hubert, and his assistant Zoe!
That's it. What I haven't told about us all—you may discover as the night goes on. Welcome.

(All performers bow to the audience.)

VIVA: Let's get the latest, shall we?

*(*VIVA *flips on the radio. Music, static, and then)*

COPTER PILOT: *(On radio, with helicopter sound)* ...still some smoke and burning down there. I'd say a helluva big meteorite—or else some campers didn't listen to Smokey.

NEWS ANNOUNCER: Thanks, Bush Ranger. We've just been in touch with the Naval Air Station and Commander Patterson stated officially that there was only commercial traffic on their radar at the time of the sightings. No unidentified aircraft. So for all you saucer buffs out there—wait till next time, and keep watching those skies.

(VIVA *turns off the radio.*)

SAMUEL: They can say that shit a million times, and it won't make it so.

HUBERT: I agree, sir. Yet it's strange how most men demand the universe be less prolific than it is. They want it smaller than their own brains, and that'd make the entire endlessly evolving creation about the size of a…

ZOE: Cue ball.

HUBERT: Their funeral, but I'd rather not attend.

VIVA: Something went down over there. The Captain saw a deer near the terminal on the other side—it had some nasty burns and blisters on its hide.

RAY: You got an intergalactic starliner, pilot checks the instruments—losing life support and going down fast. They can't make it to any civilized planet, but right nearby is this sabre-tooth backwater. The pilot figures, let's head for an unpopulated area, and we don't have the natives snooping around while we change the fan belt. Makes sense.

LILY: If they think like we do. What if the pilot is some weird *entity*, like a blob of electric jello? Or a sort of big frog thing?

VIVA: What if there's a wisp of smoke at the wheel?

SAMUEL: They took away my library card. But before this injustice, I looked into it. That we are all drawn to this place is nothing new. There is no period of human history which has not left the sort of records now called U F O reports. Sir Desmond Llewellyn produced a list of ninety-seven examples of such sightings in the eighteenth century, including the flaming cones seen over Worcester in 1761. Julius Obsequens tells of luminous flying ships over Rome, and strange women in silver clothing appearing on the banks of the Tiber. There is a papyrus in hieroglyph that claims certain slaves of the House of Isis saw a sparkling ball of light dancing in the sky above Thebes.

LILY: Tinkerbelle.

RAY: Whoever they are, they're gonna need contacts, a man on the ground, someone who understands their potential. Someone media-savvy. Lot of people would like to fuck them over.

TOM: Who are they?

RAY: Who? The space people?

TOM: The people who want to fuck them over.

RAY: Look around. I'd have their interests at heart. If they have interests. I even got a few things for them in case they're humanoid. *(Taking out stuff from his pockets)* Beef jerky. Gum. You want some?

TOM: Sure.

(HUBERT *joins them. They each have a stick of gum or jerky. Beautiful and stately music begins under...)*

HUBERT: My fellow travellers, that godforsaken smear of half-burnt forest across the river may just be the ninth wonder of the world. Our private Colossus. That site could draw fools by the millions and wise men in the bargain.

LILY: I just remembered...I have an apple somewhere in this bag. *(She digs around, finds an apple, takes out a pocket knife.)* Would anyone like some?

(Thunder, and the lights flicker.)

ZOE: Me. I would, if you please.

(ZOE makes a little curtsy, and LILY hands her a slice of apple. VIVA is handed a slice too. The women eat their apple slices. Sound of rain, more thunder, still far off. Music full, continues and ends.)

TOM: Having discovered they were all pilgrims to the same uncertain shrine, the travellers fell to talking. With Viva's urging...

VIVA: A storm is up. We're all here for the night. Our time together is a kind of gift, separate from our moving lives. I have a notion, and if you all agree, we'll pass the evening pleasantly.

TOM: All the company agrees to tell each other tales, one tale to each.

LILY: Sure.

RAY: Why not?

HUBERT: Agreed.

ZOE: I'll play

SAMUEL: Done.

TOM: So we begin. If we don't pass the time more pleasantly, at least we'll find out something new.

ACT ONE

RAY'S TALE: THE STORY OF NICK SLICK, DARLENE, RUDY, AND GEORGE THE COOK

RAY: I'll go first and then sit back and listen to the rest. My tale is simple, and, of course, its true. But I don't think I'd tell it to the kids. Excuse the bad language, please. It's the way they talk where I come from.

(RUDY *enters, an older man. He sits on couch, watches T V. On the T V, a statue of Saint Anthony.*)

RAY: Rudy's a plumbing contractor. He works damn hard and got some money in the bank. He's pushing fifty-five, got liver spots just showing on his hands. The story is, he married a young wife.

(DARLENE *enters, tight dress.*)

RAY: Rudy ate his dinner every night at the Seafood Saloon. Darlene's the hostess there and showed him to his seat. She said

DARLENE: Enjoy your meal.

RAY: One thing led to another, and here they are.

(DARLENE *sits by* RUDY. *The T V plays.* RUDY *slips an arm around* DARLENE, *tries to get sexy with her. She pushes him away.*)

DARLENE: Not tonight, Rudy honey, O K? I'm just not feeling right. Girl stuff.

RUDY: O K, baby. I'll save my loving up just for you.

(DARLENE *winces.*)

DARLENE: Why do we got that ugly statue on the T V, honey? It's always in my face when I watch my shows.

RUDY: That's Saint Anthony, baby. He's gotta be there. It's the place of honor. He protects the family. I pray to him for your safety.

DARLENE: Thanks, Rudy.

RUDY: By the way, you know that extra room we got? I rented it to this guy I met—Nick Slick. He's an actor, in a show downtown.

(NICK *appears in another space.*)

NICK: Actually, I'm just taking a scene-study class.

DARLENE: I was gonna turn that room into my dance studio.

RUDY: It's three hundred bucks a month. Besides, he's a nice, quiet guy.

NICK: I got a new Trans-Am, and I'm in the weight room six days a week. Where most people have shit *(Points to his head)*, I got what it takes.

(NICK *enters* RUDY *and* DARLENE's *area.*)

NICK: Yo, Rudy. This must be your beautiful wife.

(NICK *and* DARLENE *stare at each other. Darkness*)

VOICE OF NITECLERK: Enjoy your stay at the Quality Inn.

DARLENE & NICK: Unnnhhhh!

(Lights. A motel room. A bed. They are on it. Music, rock and roll, soft. DARLENE's *sitting on the edge of the bed, dress half on, redoing her lipstick.* NICK *still lies on the bed, shirt off.)*

NICK: Darlene, you got a face for the movies, you know that. You got beautiful tits. I want us to keep making it down here, every…

DARLENE: You crazy, Nicky? He's gonna find out sometime, and it's gonna mess me up.

ACT ONE 19

NICK: He's old, he's dumb, and he's a religious nut. Why'd you marry him?

DARLENE: You really wanna know?

NICK: Yeah.

DARLENE: He asked me. *(Beat)* Besides, he's got a hundred grand in the bank. I haven't figured out a way to get my hands on it yet.

NICK: You're gonna need a guy to party with once that money rolls in. Let Nick Slick think it over. My brain is smoking.

(DARLENE *embraces* NICK...)

NICK: Leave Rudy to me. I already got a beautiful idea...

(The Quality Inn fades, as in another area, GEORGE THE COOK *appears. He wears a chef's hat.)*

GEORGE: Welcome to your neighborhood Seafood Saloon, where every order is cooked to order by your chef, George. That's me. I can stew and bake, sauté, and fricassee. I'm a great cook, but I'm a better lover. In the trunk of that B M W parked outside, I've got a hot plate, rigged to the car battery, and a cooler full of delicacies to cook at that romantic picnic on the grass—all borrowed from the Seafood Saloon's freezer. Speaking of love, Darlene comes on at twelve...

*(*DARLENE *enters the Seafood Saloon, takes her place behind the hostess's microphone.)*

DARLENE: Mister Fripps? Fripps, party of four. Table five, on your right. Your waitress is Pam, and she'll be with you shortly.

GEORGE: She's a lollypop.

DARLENE: *(To* GEORGE, *but on mike)* Hey, Crisco, who let you outta the kitchen?

GEORGE: Darlene, please don't call me Crisco.

DARLENE: Fire me, Crisco. Make my day.

GEORGE: Darlene, how about you and me take off tonight, a romantic picnic under the stars. I'll fricassee a...

DARLENE: You gotta stop this. You know I'm a married woman.

WAITRESS: *(On mike)* Gimme a shrimp supreme and a codfish cakes.

GEORGE: Back to the fryolator. See you later?

WAITRESS: *(On mike)* Captain's platter, all the way!

(GEORGE *has to leave. He's gone.*)

DARLENE: Jerk. If I had Rudy's money, I wouldn't have to go near this seafood hell again.
Well, Nicky's working on it...

(*Back to* RUDY's *living room, with T V and the statue on it.* NICK *rises from his hiding place behind the couch.*)

NICK: And indeed I am. *(He holds up a white beard, just like Saint Anthony's on the statue. He also has a T V remote controller. He's wired a hidden C D player into* RUDY's *T V.)* We'll soon see if my performance *(Holds up remote controller)* hits the mark. *(He crouches behind the couch, ready with his finger on the T V remote.)*

(RUDY *enters, flips on the T V, sits back on the couch.* NICK *uses his controller. The video screen fills with mysterious smoke, and then the face of* NICK, *made up like the bearded Saint Anthony, appears. He speaks with a lot of echo.* RUDY *stares in amazement.*)

NICK: *(As St Anthony on T V. Italian accent)* Roooody! This is your patron saint, Anthony of Padua.

(RUDY *crosses himself, throws himself to the ground in religious awe.*)

ACT ONE

NICK: *(On T V)* You always bring flowers to church on my Saint's day, and you've been a good man and a loving husband.

(RUDY *looks up again at the screen, enraptured.*)

NICK: *(On T V)* Rooody! God is unhappy with the lustful, greedy ways of men. He is sending a great flood to cleanse the world, a second Noah's flood. It comes TONIGHT! Only one good man can be saved, in this area. You have been chosen.

RUDY: But my poor wife! Will she drown...?

NICK: *(On T V)* ROOODY! The flood tonight will be a great tidal wave. Get that old boat from the cellar up on your roof, tie it to the chimney, and when the flood comes, my son, cut the rope and you will sail safely over the great waters. Tell no one of this, not even your wife, or the Lord will doom you, along with the sinners, to a wet grave.

(RUDY *is crouched in fear before the T V, as it switches back to its usual programming as the scene fades...*)

(DARLENE *and* NICK *at night watching* RUDY. *We see them through a window. In another area,* RUDY *climbs up to the roof in a yellow raincoat, with his boat. His eye is on the sky, waiting for the second deluge.*)

NICK: *(Whisper)* He's climbing the ladder now. Call the cops. They'll see a guy sitting in a boat on his roof, babbling about Saint Anthony and Noah's flood. They'll put him in the back wards for sure, and his poor wife gets all his money.

DARLENE: *(On phone, with* NICK *caressing her)* Police? It's my husband. He's gone mad, mad I tell you. I'm so frightened... Please...7 Elm Street. Hurry!

(*As* DARLENE *hangs up, she and* NICK *embrace passionately, tearing at each other's clothes. Up on the roof,* RUDY *has fallen asleep waiting for the deluge. He snores.*)

(GEORGE *appears, chef's hat and all. He carries a large frozen salmon.*)

GEORGE: *(Calling softly)* Pssst! Darlene?

(DARLENE *appears at the window, half dressed.*)

DARLENE: Crisco? What the hell you doing here?

GEORGE: I got you a gift of love.

(GEORGE *hands her the frozen salmon. She tosses it back to him.*)

DARLENE: What the fuck would I want with a frozen fish?

(NICK, *inside, unseen by* GEORGE, *can't help laughing.*)

GEORGE: Who's that? That's not your husband Rudy...

DARLENE: Nobody. Stop acting crazy and get outta here!

(GEORGE *starts to leave, then stops and ducks down under the window. He overhears* NICK's *whisper.*)

NICK: *(Whisper)* Psst, Darlene. Call that sucker back. Tell him you'll give him a kiss, and I'll stick my ass out the window. That'll give him something to lick on.

(DARLENE *giggles, as* GEORGE *creeps away, his frozen salmon under his arm.*)

DARLENE: *(Calling out window)* George?

GEORGE: *(Calling back)* Darlene?

DARLENE: I can't let you leave without a goodnite kiss.

GEORGE: Be *right* there.

(GEORGE *returns, carrying his lit hotplate, trailing the wires to the car battery.*)

GEORGE: I'm here, Darlene. Just one kiss from your lips.

(NICK *sticks his ass out the window.* GEORGE *gleefully slams the red hot hotplate against his ass.*)

ACT ONE

NICK: WATER! WATER! I'M BURNED TO DEATH! HOLY SHIT! WATER! WATER!

(Hearing the shouts, RUDY wakes suddenly.)

RUDY: WATER?! THE FLOOD HAS COME!

(An enormous crack of thunder, penetrating the tale from the world of the ferry terminal. RUDY and his boat jump off the roof. Instead of floating on the waves, he crashes to the ground. NICK leaps out the window, holding his ass. GEORGE walks away and throws the salmon over his shoulder. The fish lands in RUDY's arms. The siren of the approaching police.)

(Final tableau: RUDY with boat and fish. NICK holding his ass. GEORGE walking away, holding his hotplate. DARLENE can't help herself. She leans out the window and laughs, and laughs and laughs.)

RAY: Nick got branded on his ass. The cook got charged with third-degree assault and did two months in county. Rudy got released from psychiatric that same day, and he's back to work at plumbing—an older, but not a wiser man. He wants her back. Darlene works as a dancer in a club downtown. Go see her sometime…

(DARLENE dancing on stage to rock music, sexy and loud. GEORGE, RUDY, and NICK watch her.)

RAY: One shouldn't be too nosy in this life
About God's mysteries or about your wife
If you're getting all the love that you desire
Of the remainder, better not inquire.

(DARLENE is gone. Music out.)

(End of RAY's tale)

VIVA: I always wondered why God didn't send a second flood—but your tale made it clear. The first one didn't change a thing. Waste of water. We're probably just as cruel, greedy, and foolish as the sinners who drowned.

SAMUEL: Though true, that's uninteresting. Now the spiral burn on Nick's rear end—that's the circle maze—both the flying disc and our search to understanding its message.

RAY: The tale's not a riddle, my friends. It's a joke.

LILY: On us. Some of us are believers—or lovers—like that husband, Rudy. You made him just a sweet-natured moron.

RAY: Think what you like, my story's done.

HUBERT: And just as well. We've had enough of love gone wrong. Let's get it right, shall we? *(He takes a small bottle out of his pocket and holds it up.)* I am an entertainer, and a spiritual pharmacist. On my tenth try, I succeeded in creating a nonstop elixir that is physical and emotional dynamite. I call it—Love Potion Number 10.

RAY: You mix that up in the bathtub?

ZOE: In the sink. Not every remedy comes from the drugstore.

HUBERT: The price is twenty dollars. Cheap for love. Slip it in her coffee. Slide it into his tea. *(Beat)* No takers? Lack of faith. Why our world is going down the tubes. Tell you what I'm gonna do. I will drop my price. I'll lose money and make friends. *(To* SAMUEL*)* Can I sell you a bottle, sir?

SAMUEL: No, thank you. I don't need that kind of thing.

ZOE: Anyone got a shovel? We better plant him deep, before he starts to stink.

HUBERT: *(To* TOM*)* How about you, my friend?

TOM: Maybe…

ACT ONE

HUBERT: Take it.

(HUBERT *hands* TOM *the bottle. He holds it uncertainly.*)

TOM: What's the price?

HUBERT: It's a gift. *(Beat)* Anyone else? Ten bucks.

(There are no takers. TOM *pockets his bottle.)*

LILY'S TALE: AT THE ZOMBIE JAMBOREE

LILY: That love potion reminds me…of another time. I had just graduated from college, and I lived in a small apartment with a roommate. I spent the time dreaming, partying, or reading the Weekly World News… *(She goes to her old apartment, picks up that very newspaper, and begins reading…)* "Amazon Woman Makes Love to Crocodile". God, these articles are ridiculous…or are they? "My Escape from Zombie Hell"…hmmm…

(LILY's roommate, SHERRY arrives, She's dressed career woman style. LILY's still reading…)

SHERRY: Lily, I've gotta get lucky soon. I had three interviews, and the assholes just kept staring down my blouse.

LILY: Yeah. Uh, Sherry, you think there's anything to this zombie business?

SHERRY: Corporate personnel directors. I'd like to take an aluminum baseball bat and a vicious small animal to my next interview.

LILY: Hypothetically, that is, I don't see why people's minds couldn't be…

SHERRY: Lily, those things are stupid. You ought to think a bit more about paying the rent, and not read those tabloids.

LILY: And maybe you ought to go out and have some fun once in a while.

SHERRY: I have fun.

LILY: Au contraire. You are living in Dullsville. Sherry, you need a break. Some guy with a neat accent asked

ACT ONE

me to this party, but I'm partied out. Here's the invite. *(Hands it to* SHERRY*)*

SHERRY: Hotel Du Temps Perdu. Maybe the drop-dead black dress...

(The Hotel du Temps Perdu. Sophisticated cocktail music. Dancing. Strange guests. Their accent is French. SHERRY *in her drop-dead dress. A distinguished gentleman, French accent,* M LAMONT*)*

M LAMONT: I can't believe it! A charming, intelligent young woman like yourself, business major in university, unable to find proper employment. You make the joke, yes?

SHERRY: No kidding. It's a bitch out there.

M LAMONT: I'm looking for someone to manage my estates—finance, export details. Sugar cane, and some coffee. But I doubt it would interest someone like yourself. The pay is only eighty thousand francs a month.

SHERRY: Uh, what's that in American?

M LAMONT: Ten grand. Of course, its in the Carribean. You'd have to relocate... *(With echo and island music)* ... relocate...relocate...

(The lights onstage flicker—then island music, stronger. Tropical sunshine. Bird squawks. The carribean. SHERRY *is at a cafe table, writing a postcard. She has a rum punch.)*

SHERRY: Dear Lily, The island of Espirito Santo is paradise. No kidding. Eden with a capital E. Hummingbirds, rum punches, and flowers everywhere. The people all seem gentle and very kind. You may not see me for...

(A blind CALYPSO SINGER *in a white suit, old guitar, and planter's hat. He advances threateningly toward* SHERRY, *singing all the while...)*

CALYPSO SINGER:
The gods got angry and the evil came
And it burned his mind in a fever flame
Over the water and onto the sand,
Life and death go hand in hand
His eyes are empty and he hates his life
And they brought him a woman to be his wife
Over the water and onto the sand,
Life and death go hand in hand
The gods are lonely and the woman is young
Give me a penny for my song is sung
Over the water and onto the sand,
Life and death go hand in hand

(M LAMONT appears.)

M LAMONT: Sherry, my dear, I want you to meet my son.

SHERRY: Sure. My pleasure.

M LAMONT: When you meet him, Sherry, you musn't stare, and you musn't cry.

SHERRY: What is he, a freak or something?

(Hypnotic drumming begins, far away. SHERRY turns toward the sound. As she does so, M LAMONT surreptitiously cuts off a lock of her hair with a large scissors.)

SHERRY: What's that drumming that goes on all the time?

M LAMONT: The work drum from the sugar mill. *(He pours something into her drink)* Drink up.

SHERRY: *(Taking a sip)* They're working at this hour?

M LAMONT: Of course. Here on the island we have a very willing workforce.

(SHERRY drinks again.)

SHERRY: Your son, is he…

ACT ONE

(The SON *appears, in a wheelchair pushed by a servant. The chair is set with votive candles: beads, feathers, juju charms. He wears a long black veil.)*

M LAMONT: A hummingbird flew in his open car window as he drove down one of our mountain roads. He was blinded and lost control. His face was burned off in the accident. People cannot bear to look at him, so he wears the veil. The accident also crippled his legs, and made him dumb. But he can understand you.

SHERRY: Hello. I'm Sherry. *(No response)* I hope we can... *(To* M LAMONT*)* What am I supposed to...

SON: Guggg gnnng.

M LAMONT: I brought you to this island to be his bride.

SHERRY: You did what?

(Drums from deep in the jungle, rhythmic and insistent.)

M LAMONT: I foresaw your reluctance. It's why I drugged your rum punch. The sleep of death is deep, and when you wake you'll give my son your love— whenever he asks.

*(*SHERRY *collapses to the floor.* M LAMONT *produces a doll, with* SHERRY's *hair. He sets it on the floor, and hands a string attached to it to his* SON. *Drums. The son draws the doll toward himself on the string, ever so slowly. Its eyes glow. As it comes closer to him,* SHERRY *rises up and also comes toward him, drawn as the doll is drawn. She stands before him, a mindless zombie slave.)*

M LAMONT: I took the spirit from her body and placed it in this shell. *(Hands doll to his* SON*)* Your wife. She is a mindless zombie slave.

SON: Gnnnng.

*(*SHERRY, *in her zombie state, walks toward the audience.)*

SHERRY: I feel no pain and no regret. I am a passenger, traveling helplessly through my own life. I soon realized the sugarcane workers were zombies as well, all dancing to the master's tune.

(Haitian carnival zombie jamboree music. Zombie Dance Number. Dance ends. Other zombies disappear.)

(SHERRY and the Zombie Master's SON alone on stage. SON beckons her to him. She approaches him in her zombie way.)

SON: *(Taking out doll)* Guunnnnng. Glllg.

(He tears SHERRY's hair off the doll. He tears the doll to pieces. As he destroys the doll, SHERRY's soul and volition come back to her. He hands her an envelope. She opens it.)

SHERRY: A plane ticket. Oh, thank you...thank you...

(The SON of the zombie master is sobbing. His shoulders heave and tears drip from under his veil.)

(Lights change, and we are back in LILY and SHERRY's apartment.)

SHERRY: And that's it, Lily.

LILY: Were you really married to that weird guy? I mean, did you...?

SHERRY: Did I sleep with him? Yeah, but that wasn't *me*.

You know—the island is really a paradise. Eden with a capital E. You ought to go there sometime.

LILY: That's a joke, right?

SHERRY: No.

LILY: But what's it *like* to be a zombie? You walk around like this?

(LILY begins to do an exaggerated zombie walk, like the ones we've seen in the Zombie Dance Number.)

SHERRY: That's not funny, Lily. There's nothing funny about it at all.

ACT ONE

(The blind CALYPSO SINGER *appears. He sings as he advances toward the two women.)*

CALYPSO SINGER: Over the water and onto the sand
Life and death go hand in hand
The gods are lonely and the woman is young
Give me a penny for my song is sung
Over the water and onto the sand
Life and death go hand in hand

(End of LILY's *tale)*

HUBERT: If that girl Sherry only had a few drops of Love Potion Number 10…pity. She'd have saved herself all that death and resurrection, de-soul and re-soul. She could have found true love in her own hometown.

VIVA: You still selling promises in my house?

HUBERT: Without success.

VIVA: You're a liar.

HUBERT: Not a very good one. I'm selling love potions on a wet night to nowhere.

SAMUEL: *(To* LILY*)* Excuse me. Your roommate, Sherry…was she actually dead?

LILY: Think what you like.

SAMUEL: Did she mention anything about the life beyond?

LILY: Look, I made that story up, O K? There was no Sherry. I never had a roommate.

HUBERT: *(To* TOM*)* See, you have to say you're a liar and a swindler. If they knew you thought you were telling the truth, they'd take you direct to the hospital for observation.

VIVA: *(To* HUBERT*)* I'd like to…

(A buzzer sounds, and the communicator light goes on, indicating a call from the other terminal across the river. VIVA rushes to the communicator, picks up the receiver.)

VIVA: Yes? ...Yes...I miss you... *(To all)* The Captain wants to talk to all of you. *(She flips a switch, static, and then...)*

CAPTAIN'S VOICE: *(On speaker)* River's all white water and running fast. Wind's strong, blowing a lot of rain. They tell me that near where that fireball came down, there's a strange slime on the trees. "Devil's jelly" they call... *(Static breaks and distorts the transmission)* ... glitters and...hideous...the rash...burning...

(Sparks, static, and an ethereal chime, and the phone connection is broken.)

VIVA: Hello? Hello? *(She hangs up the receiver.)* Line's down somewhere.

LILY: Sorry. I guess the little green men snipped the wires.

RAY: Humanoid figures in silver Spandex jumpsuits, with heads like frogs. A heat ray comes outta their eyes and zaps the cable. They turn, in kinda jerky slow motion, heading back toward their giant luminous saucer, when they confront a logger named Olaf Johansen driving a backhoe. We have Johansen's sworn affidavit that...

HUBERT: With a sex angle, we do better. Three young women are going camping, and right after undressing for bed they hear this strange whistling sound...

LILY: You guys ever think *seriously* about this? I mean, are they really from some *other world,* like some place made out of towers and glass, where really intelligent and gentle people sit around on sort of floating cushion things...

ACT ONE 33

ZOE: Or a place made of rocks and shit, without water, without sex, and without kindness.

VIVA: They're scientists, living up there in their globes of light, studying the creatures below.

RAY: Genetic experiments—make a little mutation, see if we breed true...like fruit flies.

LILY: Mister Sundown, what's your opinion?

SAMUEL: My opinion? These are the last days. We've run this game out, and it's time to pick up our check, take our hat off the rack, step outside, and look up. The lights in the sky are a sign. They mean to lead us.

RAY: Where?

SAMUEL: Here, for the moment.

(Beautiful and stately music. TOM *and* VIVA *bring from the back of the terminal a long table covered with a large, white tablecloth. They arrange seven spoons, seven glasses, and a bottle of red wine. Candles are lit. They fill each wine glass.)*

*(*TOM *brings out a stack of seven pies in tins. He puts one at each place as he talks, music continuing under...)*

TOM: Stack of pies! Discovered in the back, all apple, and not that stale, as they been sitting in the turned-off freezer.

VIVA: Poor Tom's rich.

*(*TOM *has finished setting out the pies.)*

TOM: And he invites you all to dinner.

(Everyone is seated. Rain and thunder from outside, increasing in volume and violence. Music full.)

(They raise their glasses in a toast.)

TOM: Good luck to all of you, and to me too.

(They drink. Music changes, becomes lighter in tone— ragtime piano dinner music.)

HUBERT: Ahhh. Zoe spiked that wine with a liberal dose of Number Ten. *(Silence)* Just kidding.

VIVA: Thanks to God for the apple and the baker for the pie. I'm starving.

(She eats. All eat and drink. Suddenly, a crack and a fizzle and an odd chime, and all power is gone. No lights. In the darkness...)

TOM: There go the lights.

RAY: It's love time!

LILY: Will you shut up...

ZOE: *(Howling like a wolf in the darkness)* Aaaoooooooo!

(The long table is lit by candlelight alone. They settle in again, drink and chatter. ZOE circles the table with a wine bottle and refills each person's glass. As she pours, she reintroduces them to the audience. The characters acknowledge their introductions, each in their way—a smile, a wave, a nod to the audience, taking another drink, or nothing at all.)

ZOE: *(As she fills their glasses, one by one)*
Mister Ray T Fox.
Viva.
Poor Tom.
Mister Samuel Sundown.
Miss Lily Black.
Professor Hubert.
(She doesn't fill a glass for herself. She curtsies to the audience.)
Zoe.

(ZOE raises the wine bottle in a toast. All drink, ZOE directly from the bottle.)

ZOE: Aaaaaaoooo! Story! Story!

# SAMUEL'S TALE: DR KREMSER, VIVISECTIONIST

SAMUEL: I'll take my turn and tell you of a man who probed into the secrets of the mind: Doctor Kremser, the transcendental vivisectionist.

(In another area, KREMSER *appears. Doctor's coat. He's in anguished thought.)*

SAMUEL: He waits impatiently in his laboratory. After years of research, he has conceived the surgical technique necessary to readjust the human brain for direct comunication with the upper spheres—with all those life forms that roam between the worlds.
But he must perfect the technique before operating on a human subject. His path is clear. He has to…

ALL: TRY IT ON THE DOG.

(The NURSE *appears, then exits to the laboratory.)*

SAMUEL: It's night when he comes to this decision, and the only dog available is his wife's faithful Pomeranian, Argus. The operation is performed. He sends in his nurse to observe the dog's condition.

(The NURSE *returns.)*

NURSE: The dog has gone insane. He's gnawed his own tail to bloody scrap. There's a kind of dead light in his eyes. Do I shoot him?

KREMSER: Yes. And bury him in the garden. Near the roses.

SAMUEL: This setback fails to shake Doctor Kremser's faith in himself or his greed for wisdom.

KREMSER: An animal's mind is too raw to respond. On a human subject I cannot fail.

(KREMSER's WIFE *enters.*)

NURSE: How about....

SAMUEL: Doctor Kremser's wife loves him with a deep devotion...

(She tries to embrace him. He stops her.)

KREMSER: My dear, I know I've been preoccupied, unable to give you the attentions you crave. I love you, though you do certain things that irritate me horribly. You understand my search. You hate those who mock me, who say that my work is a stupid attempt to probe mysteries no man can know.
Now the days of trial are over. I am prepared to step off the ledge into the unknown. Step off with me.
You can become the living pipeline to certain beings of the upper spheres, beings who bathe in the pregnant emissions of the lotus throne. The surgical procedure is foolproof.

WIFE: Where's Argus?

KREMSER: Argus has achieved perfect communication with certain beings. His red eyes are frozen open, never tiring of the glories before them. He...

(The WIFE *makes a break for it.)*

KREMSER: NURSE!

(The NURSE *grabs her, restrains her.)*

KREMSER: My dear, If I could perform this operation on myself, I would do so, and spare you the momentary discomfort involved. A simple rearrangement of the cranial nerves. A snip here, a snip there, a snip here, a sn...

WIFE: Listen to me, Rudolph.

KREMSER: Rudolph?

WIFE: What happened to Argus? Tell me the truth.

ACT ONE

KREMSER: He's dead.

WIFE: Did you...

KREMSER: Yes. Where you wanted him to be. Near the roses. *(To* NURSE*)* Strap her down.

*(*NURSE *does so.)*

WIFE: Must this woman assist you? I know she's never liked me.

KREMSER: She detests you, but she's devoted to science. For many years, before you came to the House of Kremser, it was she and I, buried together in our research. In her simple way, she learned to love me. Now we must say goodbye. When you emerge from the operating theater you will be my wife no longer. You will be a goddess, and your seat will be by the throne. *(To* NURSE*)* Wheel her in.

(The NURSE *wheels* WIFE *into the operating theater.)*

SAMUEL: Doctor Kremser proceeds with the preparation of—the anesthetic! Suddenly, the chemicals overpower his mind. He sees a vision of a heavenly city on an island. Temples, silent pools, gardens, with certain beings whispering to him, whispering......

(The NURSE *returns from the lab, bends over* KREMSER's *slumped form...)*

NURSE: Doctor! Doctor!

*(*KREMSER *rises, shaking off his vision...)*

NURSE: She's ready, Doctor. I shaved her. *(She holds up long hair of* KREMSER's WIFE*)* Her hair. Do I keep it for her?

KREMSER: I doubt she'll be interested in such vanities. Bury it in the garden...

KREMSER & NURSE: Near the roses.

KREMSER: Have you been in the cellar?

NURSE: Yes.

KREMSER: Is *he* there?

NURSE: Yes.

KREMSER: Did he stoke the furnace?

NURSE: Yes. It's hot.

KREMSER: Hot enough?

NURSE: Hot enough.

KREMSER: Soon all things that move between the quiet poles shall be at my command. Wait here, please.

(KREMSER *exits to the lab.* NURSE *alone on stage.*)

NURSE: Time passes...

(KREMSER *screams. He emerges, backing out of the operating room in terror. Emerging after him, the hideously bandaged form of his transformed* WIFE—*hopelessly mad.* KREMSER *buries his head in his hands. Her idiot fingers flurry in his hair. Blackout*)

(*Young* DR FELDMAN *is on the phone in his office.*)

FELDMAN: Yes...yes. The patient's quarters must be disinfected once a month. That case of lemon-scented Mr Clean is necessary equipment. Yes...yes... Listen Mr...uh, whatever your name is. I'm a psychiatrist. I can't be held personally re... Dammit! (*Hangs up, slamming phone. To audience*) Administering a small mental hospital on the outskirts of a major American city is a dead-end job for an up-and-coming clinician. Many of the cases consigned here have been sent us by the judicial system and are...rather extreme. To be blunt, the criminally insane. Despite modern techniques of probing the personality, most of them remain quite resistant to treatment. I'd be far more useful in a medical setting.

ACT ONE

(Muffled roars and growls from somewhere.)

FELDMAN: Let's be frank. I'm in kennel management. A waste of an expensive education.

(A NURSE enters. Oddly enough, this is the same NURSE who assisted KREMSER in the previous scene.)

NURSE: Doctor...

FELDMAN: Well, Nurse, you've been here a week. How does Fruitlands suit you?

NURSE: I love it here, Doctor. The patients need me.

FELDMAN: Good.

NURSE: Doctor, excuse the presumption...but you look drawn. Pallid.

FELDMAN: I have been a bit overworked lately.

NURSE: It's a shame, a brilliant man like yourself, not to have more...outlets.

FELDMAN: As a matter of fact, Nurse, a friend of mine is coming up this evening—a young woman I met in the art museum. We'll go to dinner at the inn, have a few drinks. Then we'll return and...
She should be here shortly. After she arrives, lock the outer gates, and power the electric fence. Once all is secure, take the evening off.

NURSE: There's a problem.

FELDMAN: Is it number 6?

FELDMAN & NURSE: Kremser.

NURSE: He's disturbing the others.

FELDMAN: Complex case. Seems he performed some sort of weird operation on his wife. Guilt made him crack. Well, bring him in.

(KREMSER immediately enters FELDMAN's office. He is still in his lab coat, but now it has a large number 6 on it.)

FELDMAN: Well, Kremser, you look fit. Want to borrow more surgical reference books?

KREMSER: Do you know about true love, doctor? My wife was a sacrifice—on the altar built by my blind striving to pierce the dark. Those days are behind me now. We're only men, doctor. Our life is short, and knowledge has no end. All we can do is feed, fuck, learn a few things, and die. I'm ready to accept that, doctor. That's good enough for Kremser.
I thought we might chat, doctor to doctor, about some articles in the *Lancet*. I subscribe.

(The NURSE *grabs* FELDMAN *from behind, slaps a handkerchief soaked with anesthetic over his nose and mouth. She and* KREMSER *shove him in a closet. Suddenly, there's a knock at the door.* KREMSER *opens it graciously.)*

KREMSER: Good evening.

SUSIE: Hi. I'm looking for Arnie...uh, Doctor Feldman.

KREMSER: Doctor Feldman is disciplining a patient. He'll be back shortly. I'm his associate, Doctor Kremser.

SUSIE: Pleased to meet you. I'm Susie Hawthorne. I hate to trouble you, but do you have some Tylenol or something? I have a headache.

KREMSER: How annoying...and interesting. That is, to a man in my profession. The human brain is intriguing, don't you think?

(Sound of FELDMAN, *twitching and banging in the closet.)*

SUSIE: What's that noise?

KREMSER: There's no noise. Severe headaches are often accompanied by auditory hallucination. I believe we can treat that promptly. Nurse!

(The NURSE *grabs* SUSIE, *restrains her.)*

KREMSER: Take her to the operating theater.

ACT ONE 41

(NURSE *and* SUSIE *exit.*)

KREMSER: Soon, all things that move between the quiet poles shall be at my command.

(*He exits to operate. Empty stage. Renewed sounds of* FELDMAN *trying hopelessly to escape from the closet. Lights fade…*)

(*End of* SAMUEL's *tale*)

(*The* KREMSER *lights fade, and we return to the ferry terminal and the long table in candlelight. Ragtime piano dinner music returns.*)

LILY: That's it? Mister Sundown, your story doesn't end.

SAMUEL: The lights faded, didn't they? It ends when I stop telling it.

TOM: That's the end of the telling. Not the end of the story.

LILY: Maybe so. But it's the same to me. What you tell is all the story I've got.

RAY: Unless you've heard it before. "Kremser" was my favorite bedtime story.

HUBERT: Mister Sundown was generous. We had plenty of story. Stories can't go on forever. The others just stopped at a more balanced moment. I prefer an ending in chaos and panic—our natural condition.

SAMUEL: That was not my intention at all.

ZOE: Why'd you tell us that one?

SAMUEL: I told that tale with the purpose of every storyteller. To amuse.

(ZOE *makes a little raspberry and turns away.*)

(*Thunder, louder than ever. Rain. The music changes, becomes stronger and louder.*)

(ZOE *takes up her drum, begins to beat it now and then with the thunder, dances a few steps.*)

(RAY, LILY, HUBERT, *and* VIVA *move away from the table into darkness.* MR SUNDOWN *steps away into darkness.*)

(TOM *is seated alone in the center of the long table.* ZOE *dances.*)

(*Wind, and the candles flicker. Lightning. The floor-length tablecoth begins to stir on all sides of the table.* TOM *stands. Music full*)

(*The tablecloth continues to rise and wave, a white ghost, a white magic carpet, candles riding on it, floating in the air.*)

END OF ACT ONE

ACT TWO

(A single, guttering candle in the darkness of the ferry terminal. Sound of rain. Thunder at a distance. The long table is gone. There may be people out there, but they're hard to see in the dark. Centerstage, a strange figure, and its outlines aren't human. Its head is huge, body small and slim, and its eyes glow with an eerie yellow light. It speaks [on mike], with a lot of volume and echo.)

ALIEN FIGURE: The planet Bluto needs men! Women too. I have come to earth to discover love. In exchange, I offer you our fabulous wisdom, wisdom, wisdom.

(Suddenly, full power returns. Lights)

*(The figure is revealed as an alien being about five feet tall—*ZOE's *best costuming job on herself from whatever she could find. Most of the outfit is made of a garbage bag. She's dressed as an alien creature for the polaroid flash cameras of* HUBERT *and* RAY, *who are poised, ready to shoot.)*

*(*ZOE *the Alien picks up an apple pie that remained partly uneaten and holds it up.)*

ZOE: If you refuse, I will squish your world into philosophical fragments, fragments, fragments.

*(*ZOE *squishes the pie into pieces in her hands. At this moment of demonic otherworldly triumph, the flash pix are snapped.)*

RAY: Beautiful, baby.

HUBERT: Front page, Sunday supplement.

(ZOE *flings the now-empty aluminum pie tin into the air, and* HUBERT *and* RAY *shoot flash pictures again.*)

RAY: Confirmed saucer sighting.

HUBERT: Photographic evidence!

ZOE: *(Taking off alien outfit)* I've had enough.

HUBERT: Zoe, we need more material.

ZOE: Shoot the U F Os.

(RAY *goes to a group of homemade pie tin U F Os, gets one ready to fly.*)

VIVA: Uh, those pictures are going to look like the most obvious fakes.

HUBERT: Obviously. But interesting. These photos will be colorful, stupid, yet somehow engaging.

VIVA: I doubt it.

HUBERT: The public's desire for sensation remains forever keen. A bottomless lake.

RAY: Yo!

(RAY *flings a wild-looking spaceship made of a pie tin, toilet paper rollers, and string into the air.* HUBERT *takes the photo.* VIVA *stares at them in amused amazement.*)

RAY: Viva, if that fireball's a meteorite, or a 747, then I got a load of trade garbage I can dump in the river. If it's travellers from the stars, who've come through the…the…

HUBERT: Black void of nothing.

RAY: To say…

HUBERT: Howdy!

RAY: Then they'll be so fucking hot that nobody'll care if there's some bullshit involved in their promotion.

LILY: There's a name for that.

ACT TWO 45

RAY: Acumen. Executive business acumen.

(During the following speech of TOM's, LILY *and* ZOE *listen, while* HUBERT, RAY, *and* VIVA *rig the mother ship to be photographed. This is an auto tire spray painted silver with lights and paper fittings. They get it ready to be set on fire, and crash.)*

TOM: *(To audience)* We're still here, as you can see. The weather's no better. I thought I'd start part two by telling why I live up here in the woods like a bear, and then I realized I didn't know, exactly.

I used to bum around on freights, trying to see the world from the open door of a boxcar. One time I'm under a platform in the Birmingham yards, and the Alabama State Police grabbed me. The judge booked me on a D and S.

LILY: Drifting and Spinning? Doomed and...?

TOM: Dangerous and Suspicious, and believe me I looked like a choirboy under the cinder dust. He soaked me six months—in a state waste-processing facility. That's shoveling garbage into an open pit fire sixteen hours a day.

"Get to work, dirtbags! Shovel that shit!" Nights I was so tired I couldn't sleep. I'd look up at the ceiling boards and wonder what the fuck I was doing there, and was this actually my life? In the next bunk was a tramp like me, but older—about fifty. He was a vicious, unrepentant bastard. He'd steal anyone's food. He'd brag to me about rapes he'd done. Sometimes I'd look into his sleeping face—two day's worth of beard with some gray in it, cheeks with the veins breaking through from alcohol, dirty wool cap on his head—even in his sleep he looked angry, and stupid, and crazy.

I believed then, young as I was, that we all should love one another—but this particular human being put my ideas to the test.

The day before my release, he slipped and fell into the pit fire. No one moved to hose him down. He tried to scramble up, but his clothes caught, and then he lay there in the garbage on his back, like a burning beetle, and screamed.

Finally, they hauled him out. Death didn't seem to have changed him any. He still looked angry, and stupid, and crazy. I was glad he died.

I do believe that working in that place gave me an excellent notion of what it's like for the damned in hell, if we got one.

Most days, this world is so beautiful it breaks my heart to be alive in it. And yet we live with cruelty, and madness, and death.

SAMUEL: That contradiction is called purgatory—neither heaven nor hell, but standing on one foot on the narrow rock between. That act of balance is how we live. D and S. Dangerous, and suspicious.

LILY: Doomed and sparkling.

SAMUEL: Indeed. You better not go south. They may pick you up again in the state of Alabama.

(*Upstage,* VIVA *holds the mothership as* HUBERT *sets it on fire. As these two and* RAY *make strange, alien-spacecraft noises,* VIVA *climbs up on a bench, holds the burning mothership high over her head. She drops the mothership to the floor. It goes down in flames, as* RAY *and* HUBERT *fire their flashcameras.*)

HUBERT: Cut, and print that.

(*Thunder in the distance. The sound of rain and wind is still strong.*)

ZOE: They might be lost...

TOM: Who?

ACT TWO

ZOE: Them. If they're across the river, they might be lost. Or hurt.

HUBERT: My sweet Zoe. They're probably criminals—twisted mutant starspawn.

RAY: Their sentence is a one-way ride to the most dreaded punishment in the galaxy—life on Earth.

LILY: Maybe they got their two weeks, and they're on some kind of alien package tour.

SAMUEL: In that whirlwind four living creatures, each with four faces: ox, lion, eagle, man. And around that wheel of fire was yet another wheel, a wheel in the middle of a wheel—

HUBERT: That was seen in the sky by a long-dead priest, Ezekiel the son of Buzi, in the land of the Chaldeans by the river Chebar.

VIVA: I was once at a carnival, and I went on a ride called the Ezekiel.

(The following PITCHMAN *speech begins softly, on mike, and continues under the following dialogue.)*

PITCHMAN 1: *(On mike)* See the midget bull Tiny Tim, his wife Miss Vicky the midget cow, and their cousin Miss Tiptoe, the midget goat...

HUBERT: I invented it. A wheel in a wheel, the little wheel run by faith, and the big wheel run by the grace of God.

VIVA: Soon as I got off it, I threw up.

VIVA'S TALE: OLGA THE HEADLESS WOMAN

PITCHMAN 1: The tiny trio from the farm, just like you see 'em in the pictures. They're all here and they're all alive...

VIVA: I kept walking down the midway...

(PITCHMAN 2 *appears. Near him,* LIONELLA)

PITCHMAN 2: Lionella, see Lionella, see Lionella the Jungle Girl. She's alive, living, and breathing. You'll hear her speak to you in her own peculiar manner. You talk to her, and she'll talk to you. We place Lionella on public exhibition without shame and asking no pity. This is the first and only time this show has been permitted in this state. No, she is not preserved in a bottle of alcohol. Alive, alive, alive. Take the advice of a stranger. See Lionella, the jungle girl.

Until she was fourteen she kept her secret, and then in the high school locker room, she was spied on as she changed her clothes. The entire cheerleading squad screamed in horror. The teacher couldn't put her back in the locker room with the girls, and she couldn't put her in the locker room with the boys. You'll find out why once you step inside and see Lionella, Lionella the jungle girl.

(LIONELLA *snarls. She and the* PITCHMEN *are gone.*)

(DOCTOR LANDU *appears. He stands before a painted banner: the picture is of a train that has derailed, the locomotive lying on its side, and the passenger cars scattered. Painted smoke and flames.* LANDU *needs a shave, but is otherwise complete with white coat and stethoscope.*)

ACT TWO

LANDU: Olga the Headless Woman, the ninth wonder of the world.

(LANDU *pulls the painted banner aside.* OLGA, *the Headless Woman is revealed. She is seated and wears a low-cut top. Instead of her head, there is a shiny metal cylinder that rises up from her bare neck, topped with a gauge. Into this metal cylinder run various clear plastic tubes with fluids pumping through them. The equipment looks old and worn, hoses patched with adhesive tape, cracked glass containers.* OLGA's *tubes are connected to a panel with buttons, lights, switches, gauges. A green light pulses with her respiration. An older woman,* ESTELLE, *sits in a chair near* OLGA. *She wears a nurse's cap. She knits.)*

LANDU: She lives and breathes, surgically connected to the apparatus before you.

I am Doctor Landu. Five years ago I was on my way to a medical convention when my train derailed. Corpses all over the tracks. I crawled out the window of an overturned pullman, medical bag in hand. The first victim I saw was Olga. She was lying on the ground, her skirt up around her waist. Her head was ten feet from her body, severed clean as she was flung from a window. It was just this opportunity I had been praying for. I spent the last money I had for an ambulance to rush her to a private hospital.

Even when confronted with this miracle in the flesh, many people are skeptical. They believe Olga's body is a cleverly constructed dummy. Decide for yourselves. I will now turn on the nerve exciter.

(LANDU *flips a switch.* OLGA *twitches and wriggles sexily. She almost stands. Her hands tense like claws. They relax. She is still.* GEORGE *the Cook, from the first tale, joins the group viewing* OLGA.)

LANDU: That's her aerobics class. Couple times a day keeps the muscles from going soft. This button injects liquid food into the body, and this switch is for evacuation. For a little treat, if Olga's been a good girl, we drip a quarter grain of morphine into the bloodline.

Olga the headless woman. I wrote a one-hundred-and-three-page letter about what I'd done with her to the goddamn Institute of Reconstructive Surgery and the goddamn American Medical Association. No answer. They should stick their pills up their ass, like a few thousand C Cs of strychnine in a rectal suppository. You ask me, how long can science keep her alive? Science is me. Quite a while, I imagine, if none of this equipment wears out. Olga's medical expenses have been enormous. I plunged into debt like a diver into a deep well. I have never come up. We are forced to tour. In other words, this freak I made is the cause of my poverty and the only thing between me and the men's shelter.

I have never had this level of skill again. I'm not sure why I succeeded. Maybe I was guided by love. Fucking stupid miracle. Even now I'm the only one who knows how this bunch of plumbing operates...

(*Something is going wrong with* OLGA's *equipment. Flow is erratic, gauges are dropping. She twitches erratically.*)

LANDU: Does Olga know she's alive? Depends on what we mean by "know". Without a head, those perceptions she has are totally unfiltered doses of the world, coming in direct to the skin and spine, in some delicate and monstrous way. Olga doesn't know the color of your hat, but she has feelings about you... and about me. Not feelings exactly—a complete and detailed sense.

(ESTELLE *notices the equipment problem. She stops knitting, rushes up to* OLGA. *She tries an adjustment or two. The light that pulses with* OLGA's *breathing flickers.*)

ACT TWO

LANDU: Olga the headless woman. She's the ideal wife, as she can't run her mouth at you. Ha-ha. She can write, however. The idea of localization of mental function in the brain is bullshit. Knowledge is everywhere in our bodies, in the spinal column and in the bones. Olga can write—but I don't like reading what she has to say. I don't let her have the magic marker and paper anymore.

(Gauges drop, OLGA slumps, strange twitches. The breathing light goes out.)

LANDU: You know you can do a helluva lot for a person in this life, and if they don't love you, that's not gonna make them love you, no matter what you do. That's a fact.

ESTELLE: Doctor! Olga's dying!

(LANDU turns, rushes back to OLGA, labors over readjusting the medical equipment. Panic. ESTELLE is almost in tears. Suddenly, all devices function again! OLGA straightens up, liquid flows again in the tubes... LANDU turns, sweating, to the audience. He bows. They applaud.)

LANDU: Thank you. Thank you. Now, ladies and gentlemen, before we go any further, you must admit that Olga has her charms. Even I am not immune.

(He flips the nerve exciter switch. OLGA's body writhes and twists sexily. He flips the nerve exciter off.)

(LANDU closes the painted curtain, concealing OLGA and ESTELLE from view. LANDU holds up a key.)

LANDU: Can everybody see this little key. Look at it shine. This little key opens a door—a door to a very special kind of love. The fact is, this is the key to Olga's private trailer, parked immediately behind this theatre. She's in there all by herself. I am gonna take bids for this key here and now. I make this offer without shame. What you bring back from the dead, that's yours: to keep, sell, or rent. This is an interesting proposition to the sporting young men, or women, in the audience—and one you won't meet up with every day. Do I hear a hundred dollars? What do you say? You sir, you look like a sporting man. Do I hear fifty? What do you say? Here's the key. Now what do you say?

(*No one responds.* LANDU *pockets the key, shrugs, leaves the stage. The audience, including* GEORGE *and* VIVA, *disappears.*)

(*The curtain reopens.* OLGA *the Headless Woman and* ESTELLE, *as before.*

ESTELLE: No one ever goes for that shit. It's too fucking ugly, even for Americans. He keeps trying.
That shiny key won't open anything. There's no trailer. She stays with us in a motel near the lot.
You want the truth?

(ESTELLE *carefully lifts up and removes the mirror hood that provides the "headless" illusion. "*OLGA*" is revealed. She's a young girl, and her head looks fine. She stands, looks shyly at the audience, then begins to talk softly to herself. She's what we call retarded.*)

ESTELLE: Her name's Claire. She's slow, that's all. We needed a girl for the act. Landu got her from a home—said he was her uncle to make it legal. He gave the head man there five hundred bucks, and the questions stopped. I was with him. I said I was her Aunt Martha. Just a childless middle-aged couple who wanted love in their lives.
Funny thing. We got some.
Sometimes I think Claire's a lot smarter than the both of us. It's true what he said about not giving her magic marker and paper no more, but only in the show. At home she draws pictures all the time. We used to let her write notes when she was under the hood—pass

ACT TWO 53

'em out to the audience. A souvenir from Olga. But she always wrote the same thing. I saved the last one.
(She takes a piece of paper out of her pocket and unfolds it. The letters are big and legible, in a childish scrawl. "OLGA WANTS TO DIE". *To* CLAIRE*)* Come on, honey. Let's go.

*(*CLAIRE *takes* ESTELLE's *hand. She waves goodbye to the audience.)*

CLAIRE: Bye-bye.

(They're gone.)

(End of VIVA's *tale)*

LILY: You got me crying, you know that.

HUBERT: Viva, you really think finding a little bit of happiness is so desperate, and so sad?

VIVA: The story wasn't supposed to be like that. Not so nasty, and not with all that cheap sentiment.

HUBERT: The "cheap sentiment" is what I liked. You may just have one of those stories that tells itself however the hell it wants to.

VIVA: Maybe.

RAY: I felt bad that no one grabbed the key. I thought we'd get this headless sex scene…just kidding.

LILY: I'd like to know what passion would be like—without my own head to get in the way.

RAY: Just think nothing. Then *do* it. Get loaded. Whack off. Set your car on fire.

(Mad and violent music. A frantic, desperate, and occasionally graceful dance. All dance separately and at times together: HUBERT *&* VIVA, LILY *&* RAY. ZOE *gets* SAMUEL *dancing with her. Dance and music end.)*

RAY: Lily, why don't you and me wrap our hot, naked bodies around each other and throw ourselves into the river, let it carry us down to the sea.

LILY: Ray?

RAY: Yeah.

LILY: Forget it.

RAY: You work for a fancy magazine, and I'm a bum. Is that it? You're a goddess, and I'm a...

LILY: Ray, shut up, please. I want to hear Zoe's story.

ZOE: 'Scuse me?

RAY: Lie down on this bench and let's talk this over.

TOM: Zoe?

ZOE: Somebody call me?

TOM: Your turn.

(Everybody looks expectantly at ZOE.)

ACT TWO

ZOE'S TALE: THE STORY OF ELMO MARCH

ZOE: The Story of Elmo March.

(Two narrators appear. They are BIG DADDY NITEOWL *and* KANDY KANE, *two very late-night radio talk-show hosts, with professional radio voices. They have microphones. Tables, chairs, other microphones, live radio interview paraphernalia near them.)*

(In another area, a child, ELMO MARCH, *plays a private game with a stuffed monkey.)*

KANDY: Welcome back, all you niteowls.

KANDY & NITEOWL: Hooooo! Hoooo!

KANDY: It's time for your bedtime story. Listen up. Scene One: The Vision of a Lonely Boy.

NITEOWL: Young Elmo March has wandered down to Ferris Pond.

KANDY: He's a cute kid. A little sad but really cute.

NITEOWL: He sure is, Kandy. He's playing with a stuffed monkey he just got for his fifth birthday.

ELMO: Look in the mirror, monkey! What do you see? Monkey face! Monkey face!

NITEOWL: Suddenly, he hears something strange...

(Ethereal chimes. SILVERGIRL, *a girl from outer space, appears. She wears flowy silvery stuff and looks like a cross between a sci-fi spacegirl and the princess in a fairy tale.)*

SILVERGIRL: Ellllmo! Elmo March!

KANDY: Little Elmo's never seen anything so beautiful. He's frightened, and excited.

*(*ELMO *begins to speak to the* SILVERGIRL, *but...)*

NITEOWL: Don't talk to strangers, Elmo.

KANDY: He tries to give her his monkey.

SILVERGIRL: I don't want your toys, Elmo. Where I come from, we have toys even more marvelous than your monkey. Though the monkey is pretty good.

ELMO: Where do you come from?

SILVERGIRL: That's a secret for now. I'll tell you next time we meet. Goodbye, little Elmo. Be good.

NITEOWL: And in a swirl of shining dust motes, the silver girl disappeared.

(She does. Darkness)

KANDY: Many years pass. Scene Two: Strange Doings at the Mall

NITEOWL: Elmo March is married now. He has two children, Lisa and Elmo Jr. He even owns a clock shop in the mall.

(ELMO *the adult, with clocks and watches*)

ELMO: Welcome to Tick-Tock City, where the big hand is on selection, and the little hand is on dependability.

KANDY: He loves his family, and they love him, but sometimes he can't understand why they should. *(Whisper)* Tick-tock, tick-tock... *(And on under)*

NITEOWL: And sometimes, when he sits alone in the shop, late in the evening, surrounded by the hundreds of ticking timepieces—his life seems empty, and stupid, and slow.

(A mysterious SHOPPER enters in a long coat and hat, dark glasses. Ethereal chime)

ELMO: Sorry, ma'am. We're closed.

SHOPPER: I know that, Elmo March. It's why I came so late, so we wouldn't be disturbed.

ACT TWO 57

ELMO: I have to get home and...

(*The* SHOPPER *opens her coat and takes off her hat. She has cascading silver hair and silvery, flowing clothes. It's...*)

SILVERGIRL: You know me very well, Elmo. I'm the girl from Ferris Pond.

ELMO: I've thought of you every day since we first met...but...but you haven't aged at all!

SILVERGIRL: You're right, Elmo. We don't age, but we change in other interesting ways. Once we know each other better, I'll show you.

NITEOWL: The fluorescents caught the highlights of her long, silver hair. The curves of her body were revealed by the peek-a-boo nature of her strange, shining clothing. Elmo felt dizzy.

SILVERGIRL: Can I have one of these Swiss babies? (*Pointing*) The one with the diamond chip inlay. We don't have "time" where I come from, Elmo, but I'd like the souvenir.

ELMO: Of course. (*He slips the watch onto her wrist.*)

SILVERGIRL: We have been observing you for years, Elmo, and you have been chosen. Be prepared to help us spread our wisdom and save your world from otherwise-certain destruction.

NITEOWL: Elmo swore to spread the word of the space people on earth.

KANDY: He would meet mockery and persecution.

ELMO: I am ready for all the shame and sorrow the world may dump on me.

SILVERGIRL: Good.

NITEOWL: The silvergirl kissed him gently on the cheek.

(SILVERGIRL *does so.*)

KANDY: Scene Three: The Niteowl Show, with Big Daddy Niteowl and Kandy Kane.

KANDY & NITEOWL: Hoooo! Hoooo!

(Joining them in their studio are ELMO *and* FELDMAN *from the Kremser story.)*

NITEOWL: The wisdom of the space people reminds me a bit of the golden rule, Elmo. That sound right to you?

ELMO: Well, actually, they do teach something similar, in a deeper way. Their civilization, you see, is…

KANDY: We have a little surprise for you tonight, Elmo. The gentleman seated across from you is Doctor Arnold Feldman, a psychiatrist at Fruitlands Sanatorium. We asked him to help us understand your encounters with the space people.

ELMO: It's all in my book, *Words to the Wise From Beyond the Blue*. *(He shows a copy.)* Three bucks.

FELDMAN: This spacegirl, Elmo, how do you *feel* about her?

ELMO: You're the crazy ones, you know. There's so much pain and trouble in the world. You don't need this doctor. You need to bring the President to meet me, and the Pope.
The big hand is on the human brain, and the little hand is on the stars.

NITEOWL: Scene Four: All Tangled in the Vine.

*(*ELMO *stands on a streetcorner. He tries to sell his book* Words to the Wise From Beyond The Blue. *The book has a tag on it that says: "$3.00".)*

KANDY: At first, Elmo was continually in touch with his friend from space. He had an old T V which she taught him to retune as an interplanetary communicator.

ACT TWO

NITEOWL: Unfortunately, no one believed him. Even his own family made fun of him. His wife felt sorry for him, but she left him anyway.

(*The* CALYPSO SINGER *from the Zombie tale enters. He advances toward* ELMO, *singing.*)

CALYPSO SINGER:
The saucer landed and the spacegirl came
And she burned his mind in a fever flame
Over the ozone and into space
Life and death in a terrible race
The gods are lonely and men are blind
Give me a penny for this song of mine
Over the ozone and into space
Life and death in a wonderful race

(*The* CALYPSO SINGER *is gone.* ELMO *is confused, lost. He holds up his book, still hoping for some contact or recognition.*)

KANDY: Worst of all was that for months now, the Silver Girl had stopped appearing. The interplanetary communicator stopped working. No one bought Elmo's books.

(ELMO *drops his book onto the ground.*)

NITEOWL: Elmo March gradually became convinced that he had been deluded, was temporarily insane—that he hadn't really seen anything at all.

KANDY: Scene Five: Radio Recantation.

KANDY & NITEOWL: Hooooo! Hooo!

(*Radio interview setup as before. Microphones*)

ELMO: I believe that's true, Kandy. Some kind of persistent hallucination. In a way, I dreamed it all.

NITEOWL: Now that you've understood all this, confessed it to all to the niteowls out there, do you feel a sense of relief?

ELMO: *(Panicky)* Honestly, no. I'm frightened. What if—I'm wrong? They trusted me and I denied them. I denied her...

KANDY: Easy! Elmo, honey, forget that space girl. You need some down time.

NITEOWL: There's no shame in seeking professional help if you...

(ELMO *isn't listening. He grabs a microphone with both hands, and his plea is desperate.*)

ELMO: Can you hear me out there? Does anybody hear me?

KANDY: Scene Six: At The Quality Inn.

(ELMO *and a* HOOKER *[same actress who plays the* SILVERGIRL*]. They are in a motel room. A bed. She is on the bed, wrapped in a satin sheet. A large paper bag with something in it is nearby.*)

ELMO: You're sure you're a prostitute?

HOOKER: Quite positive.

ELMO: And you'll do what I want—if I pay you?

HOOKER: I hope I will. Or we're both wasting our time and talent here, aren't we? *(She reaches for him, to take off his clothes.)*

ELMO: *(Pushing her hands away)* No, no. Don't do that.

HOOKER: *(Leaning back on bed)* O K. It's your dime. Tell me when you got it figured out.

(She takes a book out of her bag and begins reading. It's Words to the Wise From Beyond the Blue.*)*

ELMO: That book...

HOOKER: "Words to the Wise From Beyond the Blue." You into U F Os?

ELMO: I wrote that book.

ACT TWO 61

HOOKER: Sure you did. And I'm the Queen of Neptune.

(ELMO *hands her the paper bag.*)

ELMO: Wear this. (*She reaches in the bag, begins to pull out some silver fabric. She looks at it questioningly.*) It's only a dress. I made it myself.

HOOKER: That's reassuring.

(ELMO *takes out his childhood stuffed monkey. He falls to his knees, closing his eyes. He holds it out to her.*)

(*The* HOOKER *puts aside* ELMO's *dress, lets the satin sheet she has been wrapped in fall to the ground. An ethereal chime. It's the real* SILVERGIRL, *who first came to him at Ferris Pond. She looks down at him sweetly, full of kindness and love.*)

ELMO: Take it...please. Just hold it.

(*She takes the stuffed monkey.* ELMO *is crying. He turns to look at her.*)

SILVERGIRL: Don't cry, little Elmo. I love you. And you did very, very well. You did just fine.

(*End of* ZOE's *tale*)

(*A moment's silence.* SAMUEL *looks particularly weak and fevered.*

VIVA: Listen...what do you hear?

LILY: Nothing.

VIVA: The storm's blown itself out. (*She goes to the door, looks outside.*)

VIVA: It's stopped raining.

(ZOE *goes past her, out the door into the night.*)

RAY: That story got me thinking. Maybe that U F O is just our mutual hallucination...

LILY: Or a living creature, a huge glowing being of the upper atmosphere. Maybe they have a language of light, and it's when they're talking to each other that we see them in the sky.

HUBERT: Or they're something that exists beyond the five-pronged human sensorium. We see the part that registers on our screen...the tip of the tip of the tip...

(ZOE *returns.*)

ZOE: Flying saucers out there. A squadron, hovering right over the terminal.

(*No one knows whether to believe her for a moment, and then they realize it's a game, but one she's playing seriously.* ZOE *seats herself next to* SAMUEL.)

ZOE: You know, those flying things are actually God's angels. Seraphim and chubby little cherubim.

LILY: Leave him alone, Zoe.

SAMUEL: It's all right. I know she's only playing. I liked her story about Elmo March very much. You are all very kind.
Did I tell you, my name is Samuel Sundown and my ears hear the up yonder spirits, and my eyes see by the gracious light of the moon. I reached the town of Spokane, on the bus. I was stopping at the Ramona Hotel. Then I heard and turned north. I am searching for my life. I walked under the pale stars and guided myself through the night. I arrived here to join this pleasant company.
I am not going to hurt anyone. My spirit is just flying around this country like a bird.

HUBERT: Mister Sundown, go to bed. Tomorrow we'll take you across the river to the deep north woods, where the sharp cry of the crow slices the resinous murk. We will seek and we will find, and we will put the breath of life into your lungs. And Zoe will walk alongside you and hold your hand.

ACT TWO

ZOE: I will.

SAMUEL: Thank you. Though it has broken my life to get here, I don't regret it. My marks and scars I carry with me. In my heart and on my body. They will be my witness, and I will not be denied my reward.
I'm tired. Good night, all of you.

(MR SUNDOWN *moves off unsteadily toward a dark area of the terminal.*)

HUBERT: Zoe, tuck him in.

ZOE: I'll cut his throat and take his wallet.

HUBERT: No you won't. Go put him to bed.

VIVA: I'll do it.

(VIVA *helps* MR SUNDOWN *to a dim area of the terminal, where he lies down to sleep on a bench. She covers him with an old blanket. Then she sings a lullaby.*)

VIVA: (*Sings*) Don't this road look rough and rocky
Don't the sea look wide and deep
Don't my darling look the sweetest
When he's in my arms asleep

Don't you hear the nightbirds crying
Far across the deep blue sea
When of others you are thinking
Won't you sometimes think of me

Don't this road look rough and rocky
Don't this sea look wide and deep
Don't my darling look the sweetest
When he's in my arms asleep

(*As* VIVA *sings, everyone in the ferry terminal takes themselves to a resting place and settles in for the remainder of the night, except for* TOM *and* HUBERT, *who sit together at a small table with a lamp above them. At last, the singer herself is gone into the darkness as well, and only the two men at the table remain.*)

HUBERT: We two remain on watch, as our ferry terminal sails on through the darkness.

TOM: I guess so.

LILY'S VOICE: *(From darkness)* Maybe if we all can understand our ongoing search—it doesn't matter if there's a fucking flying saucer over there or not.

RAY'S VOICE: *(From darkness)* Bullshit. It matters. And get your body over here.

LILY: *(From darkness)* Jesus, can't you let up for...

HUBERT: Go to sleep! All of you.

ZOE: *(From darkness)* I would if you got me some roses for a pillow. These floorboards are hard...

(Full silence descends in the terminal.)

ACT TWO

PROFESSOR HUBERT'S TALE:
THE ADVENTURES OF BUNNY AND DICK

HUBERT: Shhhh. Now it's my turn. Listen, Poor Tom, to the Adventures of Bunny and Dick.

First we have to find them... Ah, there they are, already started. They're on a train. Bunny! Dick!

(BUNNY *and* DICK *wave to* HUBERT *from their train. They are a smiling middle-aged couple from the middle west, dressed in their best leisurewear. Perhaps they have matching sweaters. Sitting near them in their passenger car is a young woman,* DARLENE, *from* RAY's *earlier tale. Also aboard the train is a veiled man, the* SON *from* LILY's *story, sitting alone by a votive candle. He's in pain and groans softly to himself.)*

HUBERT: There's the Conductor.

(*The* CONDUCTOR *appears in his own compartment. Above his head, a small light and a small bell)*

CONDUCTOR: Hi, folks. Trouble is, Dick lost his job at the gasworks. He had a little drinking problem, and there were a few valves that got turned the wrong way. Helluva blast over there. Well, Bunny had something saved up, so they thought they'd finally do what they always dreamed of. They bought some land, way out west.

BUNNY: We're starting a town.

DICK: We can make a town that'll be friendly, and peaceful, and will welcome all the world's races and religions, the rich and the poor.

BUNNY: We've got plans for a red-brick town hall, a plaza with a bandstand, and lots of room for kids and animals.

DICK: It's gonna be beautiful. We even got a few lots marked out, the best ones, for people who've got no money at all. Bunny already...

BUNNY: I already invited people from Switzerland, and Ethiopia, and Bangladesh, and Mexico, and our own U S A. I took ads in the newspapers.
We have seeds of every kind of plant and tree we could find. We might have a lot of people to feed, and we've got a whole town to cover with trees and flowers. Dick has all the seeds in his pockets. You didn't forget, did you?

DICK: I got 'em, Bunny. Town's gonna be called...

BUNNY & DICK: Eden for Everyone.

DARLENE: Very interesting, all these plans and things.

DICK: You're a lovely woman.

BUNNY: Lovely, lovely woman. Why don't you come to Eden for...

DARLENE: I'll give it a pass. The name's Darlene. I live out by Lake Isabella. It's slow out there. You know, I saw a wristwatch the other day that records your voice—then you press a little button and it plays it back to you. Tiny, like a secret in your ear. You know what I heard myself say? "Screw a roman candle up your ass." Other things too. Filth. "Fuck me and fuck George Bush." I bet you two'd like that. If you had a talking timepiece like that, you'd like it all right. All that filth and digital readout. You'd pay money to get one, wouldn't you?

DICK: If you don't shut your dirty mouth, young lady, you're gonna hit the cinders.

BUNNY: By the way, did you just mention Lake Isabella?

ACT TWO

CONDUCTOR: Hi there again. Let's say you in the audience are actually on board this train, or rather this mockery of a train, which, though it may have some entertaining features, can't actually get you anywhere. Physically, that is.

In any case, you're on board. As you travel, the closer things are to your moving train, the faster they seem to whip by.

(Demo, as a pie tin zips across the stage rapidly, close to the audience.)

CONDUCTOR: Landscape elements at a moderate distance away seem to be moving at a medium rate of speed.

(Demo—a pie tin is carried or towed by at medium speed and at medium distance.)

CONDUCTOR: The further away things are, the slower they appear to travel.

(Demo—a pie tin going by at a great distance, at very slow speed. It keeps going throughout the rest of scene.)

CONDUCTOR: Actually, all these objects are moving at the same speed. Actually, you are moving, and they are perfectly still. Actually, the earth turns, the cacti grow, the rock dissolves, the flesh withers, the solar system careens through the Milky Way... Actually, your mind is moving, and everything else just lies there. Any questions? *(Checks watch, looks out window)* Pretty foggy out there.

DARLENE: Yeah. Lake Isabella. I live there.

BUNNY: We're neighbors!

DICK: Our land is right on the south shore of the lake.

DARLENE: The entire south shore of Isabella is a swamp. Fucking idiots. You've been had.

DICK: Real estate bastards. They'd screw their own mother. I'm sorry, Bunny. I'm gonna go back there and napalm the bastard's office...

HUBERT: Meanwhile, in the next compartment, in the darkness of the moving train, someone is ill, in great pain...

(This is the veiled SON. *He's in pain, doubled over. He reaches upward with one hand, moaning in agony.)*

HUBERT: He's trying to reach the button marked "CALL" for the conductor to get help...a doctor. He's too weak to ever reach it...and then he reaches it at last.

*(*CONDUCTOR's *emergency light lights.* BUNNY *enters the* CONDUCTOR's *compartment, looks over the situation. The* CONDUCTOR *is reading.)*

BUNNY: The conductor is in his little room, and above his head the emergency light is on, but the bell doesn't ring. A wasp has died inside the little tin cup, and blocked the little tin hammer. The conductor doesn't see the light is on. He's occupied, as the train rumbles on through the night. He's reading a book.

CONDUCTOR: *Words to the Wise From Beyond the Blue.*

(The veiled SON *stands, tries to speak to the audience.)*

SON: Gnnng. Gmmmng.

DICK: At that moment, with heavy fog on the rails, our train hits an old trestle bridge over the Echo River. The bridge gives way, and the huge locomotive dives gracefully down to the stream bottom, followed by three passenger cars. The third one, holding Bunny and me and the characters mentioned previously, also contains the baggage compartment, which happens to be loaded with cartons of highly buoyant polyethylene pellets. This car floats—and so, while part of the train sits on the dark stream bottom and makes acquaintance

ACT TWO

of the fishes, and part of it hangs half suspended off what's left of the bridge, this one car floats off downstream, light as a lark, and Bunny and me, the woman from Lake Isabella, the conductor, and the sick man with his finger on the Call button—all stare out the window at the waves.

(They do so.)

CONDUCTOR: We're highballing downstream, rushing headlong to the sea. *(Checking his watch)* Right on time.

ALL RAILROAD PASSENGERS: Bye…goodbye…bye.

CONDUCTOR: Fifty miles out at sea, and the baggage compartment springs a leak.

DARLENE: Shit on a cracker.

CONDUCTOR: The polyethylene pellets stream out behind us like a pebbly white wake. *(He walks away, spilling white pellets behind him.)* The railroad car sinks.

DARLENE: Fuck me again.

SON: Gnnnnng!

(DARLENE *and the Zombie* SON *are drowned and gone.* BUNNY *and* DICK *hold hands tightly.*)

CONDUCTOR: Bunny and Dick sink down, down into the sea, holding tight to each other in the cold of the deep. They almost drown, but at last, lungs bursting for air, they bob to the surface like tops. A little empty boat comes by.

(It does. It's RUDY's *boat, from the first tale told.)*

BUNNY: We're saved, Dick. I'm so glad.

DICK: Me too, Bunny. I didn't want you to die. I didn't want to die either, but I didn't want to be alive without you.

BUNNY: I know, Dick. A woman can tell those things. Now where in the world do you think we are?

HUBERT: Before Bunny and Dick knew it, they had landed on a sandy shore.

(BUNNY *and* DICK *land. They're all alone.*)

DICK: I don't know where we are, Bunny, but it's awful quiet.

BUNNY: Nothing but dirt and sky. We're on a barren desert island.

DICK: Bunny, it looks like Eden for Everyone may never exist.

BUNNY: It's worse than that, Dick. We'll die here.

(*A moment of despair.* BUNNY *and* DICK *hold each other close, until he begins twitching uncomfortably.*)

DICK: Bunny? I feel something funny...like things moving next to my skin...oooh ahhhh!

(DICK *wriggles around, ticklish and disturbed.* BUNNY *rushes over.*)

BUNNY: Dick! The seeds! It's the seeds, in all your pockets. They were wet for days. They're sprouting!

(BUNNY *reaches into* DICK's *pockets, and pulls out all kinds of little plants. He joins her in the discoveries.*)

BUNNY: *(Pulling out plants)* Rice, wheat, barley, tomatoes, zucchini, soybeans...

BUNNY & DICK: (*Still pulling plants out of* DICK's *pockets, socks, hair—speaking alternately and/or together*) ... alfalfa, corn, grapes, lettuce, hot chili peppers! And the trees: maple, oak, chestnut, apple, black walnut, pine, Douglas fir, weeping willow.

DICK: We've gotta get these plants in the ground, Bunny. It looks like we stay right here for a while.

BUNNY: That's fine with me, Dick. Besides...I didn't want to tell you before we were settled. I'm pregnant!

DICK: Bunny...

ACT TWO 71

BUNNY: Dick...

(BUNNY *and* DICK *embrace. They are gone. A modern* LIBRARIAN *with glasses appears.*)

HUBERT: A thousand years later. Bunny and Dick have rotted away. Their bones are dust. Civilizations have come and gone on this sandy shore, but now a great and peaceful city stands there, with people of all races, temples of all religions, gardens, trees, flowers, and fruit. Do they remember? Why don't you ask the librarian?

(TOM *hesitates to enter the story, but he does so.*)

TOM: Excuse me.

LIBRARIAN: Shhhh.

TOM: *(More softly)* Sorry. Do you have a history of this place?

LIBRARIAN: Of course.

(*She picks up an old, leather-bound volume. She blows the dust off it, and this dust glitters in the light. She opens the book.*)

LIBRARIAN: *(Reading)* Our world, Eden for Everyone, was founded, of course, by that extraordinary couple, Bunny and Dick.

(*Music.* BUNNY *&* DICK *appear. They dance in each other's arms, sweetly and beautifully, as the lights fade.*)

(*End of* HUBERT's *tale*)

TOM: Why were Bunnny and Dick saved when the others in the railroad car drowned?

HUBERT: Their perfect virtue rewarded? Dumb love? Dumb luck? The hand of fate?

TOM: You told the story.

HUBERT: Doesn't mean I know why things happen. I just spoke, and they were saved.

VIVA: *(From darkness)* Is it salvation you two are babbling about?

SAMUEL: *(From darkness)* Go to bed. Salvation is under the covers.

TOM: You know, I used to bum around a lot, riding the freights. I had no home—a sort of a floating spark of life on the railroad. Even after being here five years, sometimes I wake up in the middle of the night, go to the door of the terminal, ease it open, look out at the road, and think—"What are we stopping here for?"

HUBERT: Dumb love. That's what it is. Good night.

(HUBERT *goes off into the darkness. He's gone. We can see the figure of* ZOE *moving among the sleepers. She nears* RAY.)

ZOE: If you're awake enough to hear me—you're awake enough to buy. Love Potion Number 10 powers up your dreams. The price is high. One hundred dollars a bottle.

RAY: Kid, you actually got some brains. That's a gift. Why don't you use it and get yourself some kind of life?

ZOE: How many bottles for you, sir?

LILY: *(From darkness)* Does her mother know she's up this late?

RAY: I'm going to sleep. Worry someone else with your nonsense...

(ZOE *goes to* TOM, *who sits alone under the light at the table. She sits down, puts a bottle of Love Potion Number 10 on the table.*)

ZOE: Some love drug?

(TOM *reaches in his pocket, places the bottle of Love Potion Number 10* HUBERT *gave him earlier on the table as well.*)

ACT TWO

Pilgrims of the Night was mine, all in all. Now it's ended, and the turn is yours. Tell your own tales to each other, and make those nights before you sail go by with more delight. Thank you, and to all a good night.

ZOE: Good night! Sleep tight. Pleasant dreams. *(She blows the audience a kiss.)*

(Music, and out)

END OF PLAY